An Honest Answer

An Honest Answer

poems

Ginger Andrews

Story Line Press | *Pasadena, CA*

An Honest Answer

ISBN 978-1-58654-066-1 (tradepaper)
978-1-58654-088-3 (casebound)

The National Endowment for the Arts, the Los Angeles County Arts Commission, the Ahmanson Foundation, the Dwight Stuart Youth Fund, the Max Factor Family Foundation, the Pasadena Tournament of Roses Foundation, the Pasadena Arts & Culture Commission and the City of Pasadena Cultural Affairs Division, the City of Los Angeles Department of Cultural Affairs, the Audrey & Sydney Irmas Charitable Foundation, the Kinder Morgan Foundation, the Meta & George Rosenberg Foundation, the Allergan Foundation, the Riordan Foundation, Amazon Literary Partnership, and the Mara W. Breech Foundation partially support Red Hen Press.

Second Edition
Published by Story Line Press
an imprint of Red Hen Press
www.redhen.org

In Memory
Frank Dearstine
Francis Almeda Dearstine
Tana Rae Dooley

Contents

PART THREE:

WHAT THE CLEANING LADY KNOWS

PART FOUR:
NOT SLEEPING TOO GOOD MYSELF

a prearranged agreement for no life support

An honest answer is like a kiss on the lips.

—Proverbs 24:26

A Whole Life

The presiding spirit behind Ginger Andrews' first book An Honest Answer must be William Carlos Williams. When he said he wrote in the speech of Polish mothers, he could have included the American working class anywhere. They sinewy resilience of Andrews' individual poems honors the tradition of his free verse lyrics. She listens for the poetic measure in American speech and reproduces it in unique forms. I would venture to say that the poetry of Ginger Andrews is as close to the tradition of Williams as American free verse has ever been.

Where Andrews' poems seem fragmentary at times, like those poems of Williams which Robert Frost called "snippets of things," they are in fact parts that stand for a whole, as Frost himself said any poem was—a part that stood for a whole. In Andrews' case each part stands for a whole life. That life in An Honest Answer follows a narrative arc: the early death of her mother, the illness and eventual death of her father, and the effect of these losses on herself and her surviving siblings. The operative word here is survivor. That word, used loosely twenty years ago about upwardly mobile young people, applies to Andrews: she's a survivor, saved, apparently, by her faith and her poetry. She is never just marking time, never boring, never setting herself a mere exercise. She is acknowledged among her family and friends as their poet, recorder of life and hard times in the lumber towns of the Northwest, where astounding natural beauty is no remedy for the grim facts of joblessness, alcoholism, crime, disease. Andrews shows how poetry breaks through the dank fog of these troubles, as surely as her profound and durable faith.

As the voice speaking to us in these poems, it is as fresh as Ray Carver's seemed 25 years ago. Another poet who comes to mind is her fellow Northwesterner Vern Rutsala, himself a descendant of Williams who, like Williams, has kept his eye on the working poor throughout his career. Andrews is a working class, born again Sappho, an Ahkmatova who cleans houses and teaches Sunday School. These figures come to mind not for the sake of hyperbole, but to help understand the originality of this new and remarkable poet. We glimpse one vital source of her imagination in the opening of "Home Alone":

> Cigarette smokers,
> sweet tooths,
> alcoholics, teetotalers,
> bad cooks, good cooks,
> food stamp recipients,
> low sugar & type 2 diabetes,
> depression, codependency, cancer,
> high energy, low self-esteem,
> nap takers, neat freaks, control freaks,
> carpal tunnel syndrome,
> strong arms, skinny ankles, pot bellies,
> public speakers, introverts, braggers,
> blue eyes, long legs, red necks,
> enablers, naggers, whiners,
> pride, guilt and honesty all run in my family.

And she adds, "There's never a dull moment, though I'm praying for one." Ginger Andrews speaks to us genuinely and passionately from firsthand experience, and in doing so, she speaks for others who share that experience and share it every day.

—Mark Jarman

PART ONE

ROLLS-ROYCE DREAMS

The Day I Looked In The Mirror
And Saw Nothing

It was late afternoon. Ninety-plus degrees in Dillard, Oregon.
Dad was pulling green chain at Hult Lumber Company.
I'd been missing Mom real bad, but remembered her last days
Of pain, how cancer made her cry out, and I knew
There was no pain in heaven.
My three oldest sisters were married and gone.
My sweet, habitual offender brother was doing time
For some stupid parole violation.
There was just my sister Mary Beth and me at home.
She was playing Credence Clearwater Revival's *Proud Mary*
On our cheap stereo.
I was wondering what we'd cook for dinner
Besides canned soup. And I was wondering,
Being thirteen and all, if I'd ever get any breasts.
My older sisters wore 34B or C or *D*.
I thought I'd just lock myself in the bathroom
And check to see if maybe
I'd grown a little bit.

ReClassified

WW II took just about any man,
but Dad couldn't see too good
out of one eye, was blind in the other,
had high blood pressure,
three kids and a wife.

They bused him
from Jefferson Barracks in Saint Louis
back home to Gideon
where he worked at a box factory
making just enough money to feed his family
and keep a roof over our heads,

and where some folks called him
a 4-F son of a bitch.

First Love

In sixth grade
There was a boy I liked.
He liked me too. I could tell.

His mother was room-mother
at our school parties.
I was jealous
because she was pretty,
brought fancy store-bought treats,
and because my mom had to go to heaven
the summer before I started fourth grade.

He lived four streets up from me
in a beautiful house
with a trimmed hedge
and a painted gold picket fence.

I lived in an ugly house
(I hoped he's never see)
With faded gray siding
and grass that needed mowed.

Playing tag with my sister
in our front yard one day after school,
I saw him across the street
at the neighbor boy's house.

I waved and said *Hi*.
He said *Hi*.

But he didn't wave back.

I went inside and watched him
till he rode off
on his shiny new red bike.

The next day at school
he was friendly,
but not as friendly as before.
And that's my first love story.
There's nothing more to tell.

Milk Cow Blues

I never once saw Dad kiss Momma.
Never even saw him hold her hand. But
he sang her a song about a milk cow,
how he was havin' to go without both milk and butter
ever since his milk cow'd been gone:

> *If you see my milk cow,*
> *pleeeease send her on home to me.*
> *I ain't had no milk or butterrrrr*
> *Since my milk coooow's been gone.*

Sometimes he sang the song over and over.
His voice would crack flat
when he tried hitting the high notes.
Momma's shoulders would shake.
She'd tuck her chin to her chest, reaching
to wipe tears from her eyes with the corner of her apron.
It had to be
Some kind of love

Rolls-Royce Dreams

Using salal leaves for money,
My youngest sister and I
paid an older sister
to taxi an abandoned car
in our backyard. Our sister
knew how to shift gears,
turn smoothly with a hand signal,
and make perfect screeching stop sounds.

We drove to the beach,
to the market, to Sunday School,
past our would-be boyfriends' houses,
to any town, anywhere.
We shopped for expensive clothes everywhere.
Our sister would open our doors
and say, *Meter's runnin' ladies,*
but take your time.

We rode all over in that ugly green Hudson,
with its broken front windshield, springs poking
through its back seat, blackberry vines growing
through rusted floorboards;
with no wheels, no tires, tailgates busted,
headlights missing,
and gas gauge on empty.

Love Poem For My Brother

You were so cool,
So handsome in a white T-shirt,
penny loafers and tight jeans,
driving that beat up Ford
with reversed shackles.

I gave you the big green stuffed snake
I'd won at the school carnival
to put in the rear window dash.
You told me I was a good girl.

I remember Momma crying
when Dad beat you with a garden hose
after you broke in Barview store
for beer and cigarettes,
when you went to Maclaren School for Boys,
and when you did time at the Oregon State Pen
for something statutory. Everybody said
she lied. I'm sorry you were up there
when Momma died.

Blessed Gospel Light

A full-bore black-out alcoholic
from the time she drank her first beer,
she lost a lot of good years,
passed by marriage proposals
from good-looking men
in three-piece suits
with cars and houses
already paid for, to marry
a no- 'count demented drunk
who swore his favorite song
was *How Great Thou Art*
with one hand on his heart,
the other tucked inside the top
of his too-tight button-fly 501 blues.

She worked her way up
scrubbing floors, making beds,
waiting tables, tending bar,
to hit rock bottom one cold night—
beaten half to death by small town cops
in a big city way.

Reading AA's big blue book
with one eye—the other swollen shut—
lying stiff, broken, blood and beer-stained
on a jail cell bed, she cried
while quietly praying out loud
to the heavenly higher power

A Sunday School teacher now—
she traded in her booze for a Bible,
honky tonk days for the Better Way,
the Truth, the Life.
There's a Glory that shines about her.
Ask her, and she'll tell you:
It's the good Lord shining,
It's the Blessed Gospel Light.

December Morning

Drinking Chase & Sanborn
from unmatched cups
without saucers
on a cold December morning
at my sister's place
on her first day off in quite some time,
we talk

about growing up poor
but happy as ticks
how we still ain't got much,
but we don't care.

So we both dropped out of school.
I got married & had babies.
She got drunk & stayed drunk about eight years.
We add up broken dreams & hearts
and my sister wins.

We pretend we're sipping
General Foods International Coffee—
Café Francais. I tell her
Jean-Luc thought I was cute,
but thought she was the prettiest
thing he'd ever seen.

And we talk
about how she doesn't drink anymore,
and me, finally going back to school.

We raise our coffee cups
and clink them together across the table,
Little fingers held high.

Don't Know Much About Algebra

All through grade school
I thought if I was *really* smart,
everybody would love me.
I had to fake it in math.
By the time high school rolled around,
in order to keep up appearances, I signed up for algebra.
About two weeks later, I snapped, admitted to the teacher
and whoever else cared, that I didn't get it.
There was this blue-eyed senior jock who played drums
and had an eye for me. We ran off and got married.
I got pregnant on my honeymoon night in a cheap motel
    in Reno,
had morning sickness, dry heaves, for two solid months.
It was nice though, I told myself, to be out of my dad's shack.
where the toilet never flushed and the place always smelled
like Salem cigarettes.

The Housewife

sits on her carefully made bed.
Her blue curtains are more than half drawn.
All household members are acting perfectly rational.
So everyone is a little boring.
So everyone is a little crazy.
She could pick up
her somewhat expensive marble-based candelabra—
and throw it out her window
because she's bored,
because she's just a little crazy.
For any one of a hundred reasons,
she could throw it.
But she won't.
She'll straighten the bed-covers
and, maybe, later,
she'll burn the hell out of dinner.

Come to Papa

Sitting in a rusty-armed lawn chair
In Dad's overgrown backyard, worried sick
Over what direction my life might take. Afraid
to burden this dying man, afraid he'll tell me
I've made my bed and I'll have to lie in it, or preach
about how folks with good common sense know better
than to jump out of a fire and into a frying pan.

We sit quietly till he looks me straight in the eye, slowly
crosses one skeleton-thin leg over the other, and says, hell
is being old, sick and alone. He offers the other half of an apple
he just can't eat. But Dad, I say, it's rotten
    For chrissake kid, cut out the bad part.
    If you had the brains of a peckerwood
    I swear you'd fly backwards. Just because
    you have shit running down one drawer-leg
    doesn't mean it's running down the other

Divorce Poem

You got the house
with double car garage,
work bench and tools

the kitchen
with solid oak cabinets,
built-in stove, dishwasher
and garbage disposal

one and three-quarter baths
with heat lamps, fans,
and full length mirrors

the music room
with stereo, AM/FM
tuner, equalizer,
Infinity speakers,
keyboard, microphones,
all the records,
all the tapes,
and the ten-piece
top-of-the-line
Rogers double-bass drum kit

the family room
with custom-made drapes
and the floor-to-ceiling
solid-rock fireplace
half the furniture,

half the linen,
half the dishes
half the pictures on the walls

the thirty-five millimeter
camera with telephoto lens
and tripod

the 5.6 acres,
water rights to the creek,
the grass, the trees,
the flowers
and the dog

the lawn mower
and the rototiller

the blue Chevy
short-bed pickup truck
and my ex-best friend.

I got both our boys.

PART TWO

O THAT SUMMER

Before Our Divorces

when my sister was tending bar weekends,
drinking, or snorting a line most days, she'd call
knowing my husband was at work,
that he didn't like her, and couldn't understand
why I loved her like crazy. He thought
we were complete opposites, and I agreed,
being a Sunday School teacher and all.

After our divorces
when she'd stopped drinking and I was considering it
and a possible affair, though I couldn't imagine
who would want me, she'd call or drop by
to water my plants, tell me I was crazy,
ask if I was going to church Sunday,
did I have an extra pair of panty hose, a dress,
and a dadgum freaking pair of heels
that she maybe could borrow.

I Tell Them I'm a Bible School Teacher

I tell my old friends that I'm a housewife / homemaker,
still a small town girl. Finally got out of Charleston,
never dreaming I'd be back.

> *. . . Say you're about, what, thirty-four*
> *thirty-five now?*

I tell them that I was married at sixteen
for twelve, almost thirteen years. Divorced.
Remarried about four years ago now.

> *So you married another Mike?—*
> *The one from Barview—Tarheel Road—*
> *That Mike? Well how 'bout that.*

I say my oldest sister's still here,
in North Bend now. She's the mayor's wife.
I say Mary Beth's a recovering alcoholic,
that she's still the prettiest one,
that she still tells me what to do.

> *Is your Dad still around?*
> *What about your other sisters?*
> *And where in the hell is your brother now anyway . . . ?*

I tell them I'm a Bible school teacher
At the North Bend Church of Christ.

But I don't tell them
how the kids in my class
love to march in the infantry,
or how beautiful their little voices sound
when they sing "Jesus Loves Me" off-key.
I don't say
that they too could hear them sing
if they happen to pass by Broadway Street
on any Wednesday night.

And I say I'm crazy
Not to tell them that.

On Certain Sunny Sundays

On the way to K-mart
after church services,
we pass by a tight-bunned,
blue-eyed, hairy chested
construction worker
and start talking dirty
(like only two sisters can)
and we laugh and laugh
almost going off the road
and my sisters says that we are so bad
even God doesn't know
what to do with us—
and what a scary thought that is.
But we laugh and laugh
until we cry and cry
because we're getting older
and aren't nearly as pretty
as we used to be
and because we act so stupid and silly,
struggle with our teenagers,
jobs, periods and prayers.
And we cry
because we love each other
like only two sisters can
after church services
on the way to K-mart
on certain sunny Sundays.

Friday Night

My oldest son called.
He's working full-time,
Got his own place now
And taking some night classes at UCC.

At 9:30 my sixteen-year-old son
(they tell me he's an angel)
kissed my cheek goodnight.

You bought me my favorite perfume
on Mother's Day.

Dinner's dishes are washed
and put away.

The house is clean.

All our bills are paid.

          If I drank

I guess I'd go get drunk.

O That Summer

my sister and I
both wound up back in Coos Bay
basket cases, lonely as hell.
She was recovering from drugs and alcohol,
I was newly divorced, a Sunday School Teacher
with no job skills whatsoever
and two little boys to feed,
praying for a maid job at Best Western.
Lord how we prayed

Walking from one end
Of Sunset Beach to the other, barefoot,
Freezing in tank tops and cutoffs,
Hair and makeup perfect,
Fingernails painted with three coats
Of Wet'n Wild, hoping
some good looking single doctor
was walking his dog nearby
should one of us happen
to slice our foot on beach glass

Evidently, She Says,

she's looking for a man physically
and /or mentally abused as a child.
He has a sad but sexy smile,
long eyelashes,
and wears Levi's exclusively.
He works hard
when he works.
He draws maximum unemployment benefits
whenever he's laid off. He has been
married two or three times, is currently
behind on his child support payments
but should be back working any day,
plans to get caught up,
is good in bed,
smokes pot, drinks beer, does drugs,
presently has no transportation,
and is obviously in need of a good home-
cooked meal.
She's looking, she says,
For a sick man.
The sicker, the better.

Cruising the Slammer

I am talking LOW self-esteem, this pretty woman says,
At one point I'd call up a man, invite him over knowing
the only thing I could count on from the long-legged
    Good-looking jerk
was a lay.
Oh Honey, this other gal says, I used to cruise
the county jail with my girlfriend. She'd toot her horn
to get the guys' attention through the barred windows.
When they'd wave back I was sooooo thrilled!
But hey, my friend was worse off than me,
she actually wrote them letters.

Prayer

God bless the chick in Alaska
who took in my sister's ex,
an abusive alcoholic hunk.
Bless all the borderline brainless ex-cheerleaders
with long blonde hair, boobs,
and waists no bigger around a coke bottle
who've broken up somebody else's home.
Forgive my thrill
should they put on seventy-five pounds,
develop stretch marks, spider veins,
and suffer through endless days of deep depression.

Bless those who remarry on the rebound.
Bless me and all my sisters;
the ball and chain baggage
we carried into our second marriages.
Bless my broken brother and his live-in.
Grant him the SSI. Consider
how the deeper the wounds in my family,
the funnier we've become.
Bless those who've learned to laugh at what's longed for.
Keep us from becoming hilarious.
Bless our children.
Bless all our ex's,
and bless the fat chick in Alaska

Necessity

You need to live
near the edge of the world
on Broadway Street in my small port town.

You need sweet neighbors
who grow pale pink fuchsias under Plexiglas,
and bright red and yellow dahlias—right up through gravel.

You need four sisters
who are as kind hearted as mine,
and think every poem you write is perfect.

You need an alcoholic brother
who's seen the inside of hard time,
whose blue eyes look just like yours.

You need a mother who died young,
a mother who cooked the best plain brown beans in the whole world,
a mother who taught you to share, made you feel rich
though you were poor.

You need a mother
who showed you where wild tiger lilies grow,
a mother who dressed you and your sisters
as pretty as she could for Jesus.

You need a foulmouthed old fart for a father—
who makes you laugh.

You need my dunes, my trees, my ocean,
my fog and routine rain.

You need my modest, middle-class income home.

You need my trusty, rusting '84 Ford
whose odometer reads one-hundred
and twenty-six thousand miles.

You need my $7.50 an hour house cleaning jobs,
Tuesdays through Fridays.
You need to pull weeds and trim your laurel hedge.

You need to live on the edge of the world
and, oh, how you need Jesus.

My Sister Calls

to say she's lost weight
and her old jeans fit again.
She says it's kinda neat
having her whole system screwed up
from falling out of love,
that it's not much different
than falling *in* love,
not that she's in any hurry.

Her check garnishment ends
on the 21st, and would I like to go
to garage sales with her that weekend?
She's got an antique dealer coming
sometime this morning
to buy her dark wood dresser
with the mirror. She's afraid
she'll let it go
for far less than what it's worth
but she didn't really call to complain,
she wants to know
if I've written any good poems lately
and I tell her I'm writing
just as fast as I can.

A Place Prepared

It's such a sad world.
Don't we all get on with it though?
I, for example, am upset
because I've lost a shoe
and am tearing up
an almost clean house to find it
so I can run to the store for carrots.
I have everything else I need
for a chuck roast dinner,
went to the store last night
and bought half a dozen
unnecessary things, but forgot my carrots.
Can you believe it?

I've got a sister
saving up money she doesn't have
for a divorce she doesn't want,
another sister praying
'cause she's been there. My dad's feet
are turning black from diabetes,
and about half the people I know
are recovering from an addiction.
The other half are in denial.

I've been trying to read
three chapters from the gospels every day.
I'm twenty-seven chapters behind.
                    But I believe
that all my poems are prayers,
that it's OK to ask God for anything, anytime;

that it's OK to sit down
in the middle of your floor and cry
because you've lost a shoe,
that it's OK to ask Him
for a glimpse
of what it will feel like
stepping into that place
He's promised to prepare.

Way Past Dancing

It doesn't bother him that he can't get it up anymore.
Old age and diabetes will slow a man way down, and besides,
Sex is for young folks, and Lord knows he had his share.
Never had any complaints either. Getting women was easy
If you were the only guy for miles with a Model A Ford,
And, if you knew how to dance.

His legs are numb, his feet are swollen.
Imagine, he says, *having to sit to piss.*

Swatting flies on the back porch, I ask, *Dad, are you hungry?*
He pops out his upper teeth, shows me where they broke
Night before last when he was trying to eat peanuts,
How he's fixed them good as new with Crazy glue.

An Early Spring

We've all been devastated
since week before last
when my husband's best buddy took his own life.
Thirty-eight years old. He wasn't even drunk..
We can't imagine what we'll do with his mother.
We're just sick

about the earthquake in Japan, tired of O.J., cold rain
and Jehovah's Witnesses knocking
asking questions like, are you suffering from burnout?

This last divorce has all but done my sister in.
Her big old red Ford sits broken down
under our carport, finally out of the rain.
Mushrooms grow on its back floorboard.
My sister plans to stay just till she's back on her feet.
Her five-year-old spoiled brat of a kid
calls me Grumpy Old Aunt Gin,
tells me she misses her Daddy
and that she's scared bad of her Uncle Mikey
'cause he makes her mind.
She's into my underwear, my makeup—
I can't find my blush anywhere.
She asks endless questions like, does Jesus have a girlfriend?
Today she handed me a just-picked bouquet of daffodils,
said she got them in the neighbor's yard.

Lollapaloser

So your second marriage
is not sad.
You are not drunk
on half a bottle of warm Zima
and your children
are at home cleaning their rooms.
You are not parked in a mud hole
twenty miles up Coos River
listening to Dwight Yoakam's
A thousand Miles From Nowhere.
You are not in any pain
and no one has ever done you wrong.
You have never suffered
from carpal tunnel syndrome,
bled irregularly,
or survived a butt-first breech delivery
when your first child was born
just prior to
C-sections becoming commonplace.
You refuse to feel sorry
for thirty-eight-year-old
mid-life crisis participants
who find themselves temporarily
in love with any child who looks lost
or any man who looks lonely.
You have never had a cold heart
or a weak faith.
You are not drunk.
No one has ever done you wrong
and oh sure

you knew
that your father was only teasing
about your being the milkman's daughter.

Warning

My sister tells me that people see it.
Men, especially.
It's that little lost look of yours,
saying you're not quite happy. In fact,
she says, I'd go so far as to say you project it.
I know it's unintentional.
You're a dedicated wife.
And when people see
your commitment to God
they're in awe of you. But
I'm telling you, she says, you've always had
that look, and, that figure—
the best figure of all us girls—
that waist, that butt,
and those eyes.

Almost

I forget
that my stepdaughter's not
quite mine,
that I have an ex
who married my ex-best friend,
that they have a baby daughter now.
I forget
That I'm living in a half-world.
My son,
When he laughs out loud
or tips his head to one side, almost profile,
looks exactly like his father.

Sister Ritual

Every morning I
call Mary Beth, Bob Etta, and Donna June. Usually I
call Mary Beth first. When her phone's busy I
call Bob Etta. If she's busy I
know she's probably talking to Mary Beth, so I
call Donna June. If her phone's busy I
figure she's trying to call me, so I
hang up. Wait a second. Push redial. If I
get a second busy signal I
try Mary Beth / Bob Etta again. If they're still busy I
call Tana Rae long distance. If she's busy I
eat breakfast.

This Poem

Some minor family crisis last night
that I've already put walls up around.
Some little denial game probably,
the way my legs are crossed at the knees
with my right foot wrapped tight
around my left ankle, pretzel-like,
to where it would be too much trouble
to untwist and reach across the stack of self-help books
in order to change my radio's station
which apparently has been switched from blues to gospel
by some family member who knows
I'd rather not have them messing around my writing desk.
The wrong music can throw you off track. Or maybe
it's my unmade bed, the dust on my banker's lamp,
or this foggy August morning. Maybe
it's trying to write serious poetry
when you're out of Kotex and your coffee's cold. Maybe
it's trying to convince yourself that you are not this poem,
that there will be a surprise line that you didn't know
you had in you. Maybe it's my sister
who's been diagnosed with inoperable cancer. Maybe
it's having solid white hair years before turning forty,
Nice 'n Easy's copper auburn stains
under your fingernails every month.
Or the way my legs are crossed, my toes turning blue.

Carrots in the Rain

I'm in the driver's sear
Of my sister's '78 Ford
because she can't see to drive
after dark. A whole carload of us
has just come from visiting our dad
who's dying with liver cirrhosis
and terminal stubbornness.
I'm waiting with four sisters and one aunt
in an almost empty restaurant parking lot
for another sister to get off work,
the sister who's recovering from cancer
while washing dishes at the local greasy spoon.
We see her coming from around back and holler,
Hey, Tana Rae!
She has this little square Styrofoam container,
She opens it up and asks if we want a carrot.
She gives us each one. We crunch and talk,
Decide to go somewhere for coffee.
Learning against the car's passenger door,
Tana Rae digs in her purse for her keys
because she can't fit in our car with us. We laugh.
Sitting scrunched in the old Ford crunching
Our leftover crinkle cut carrots, we laugh.
It starts to rain. Waving her carrot stub wildly,
One back seat sister leans forward
And asks if I'm gonna write a poem about this.

Good News

I've got to write a letter, card or something, anything,
to the cutest, sweetest married couple I've ever known
who took me and my boys in when I had divorced and had my
 hell year.
I read in the paper today that they've filed for divorce.

Oh the beautiful car
that I practically gave away to my youngest son
that got its whole front end smashed when he hit that deer
on Highway 38, cruising at about 75 mph.

I get away to drink a triple shot mocha
with two writer friends, one of whom has a brain tumor.

Then there's my dad, desperate with no pain medication,
dying at home. He broke his ankle last week. He offered
me six hundred dollars to stay with him till he dies.

I've got a pap test scheduled for next Tuesday,
sure enough, the same day my sister starts her chemotherapy.
Good news: my oldest sister checked,
found out that the local American Cancer Society
will fit her with a wig, one that matches her hair color,
and gave her a couple of turbans for free.

Growing Old Near Charleston

I'm still a Fossil Point kid,
poking stiff seaweed
into pale green anemone,
prying starfish over onto their backs.
I'm still afraid of half-dead crabs.

I remember crashing into cold waves
at Sunset Beach, in fog, barefoot—
because my sister did—
and spitting salt water.
We bought taffy at the Shell Shop,
Charleston Chews at Davey Jones Locker,
and candy cigarettes at Barview Store.

Wearing warmer clothes these days,
I watch waves break from my car window,
eat clam chowder and drink coffee.
Sunny days I search for whole sand dollars
and blue beach glass,
finding only broken pieces.

Bunny Arkansas Days

I want to write about Bob Etta,
Donna June, Gary Lee, Tana Rae, Mary Beth and me.
I want to write about Bunny Arkansas days,
Gideon Missouri, Flint Michigan, and Tenmile Oregon.
I want the cat off my lap, my dishes done, my headache gone.
I want my husband's fishing pole off the dining table,
his sandshrimp back in the sand.
I want my oven cleaned,
my kitchen floor mopped.
I want somebody else
to pick up every single pile of dog crap in the backyard.

I want to write about Olalla Road, Pierce Point,
blackberries and possums.
I want to know why
I let my sisters talk me into helping them move my
        antique dresser
out of one sister's house—
I can't believe I let her have it in the first place—
and up into the back of my husband's very high
four-wheel-drive-truck,
then across town to another sister's house, all the way up
her stairs, then sideways into her tiny bathroom,
only to have her decide that it doesn't look quite right,
        then back
down the stairs, back up into the truck

to finally wind up back where it started—my house,
where it no longer fits because I of course replaced its
    empty space
with another dresser.

I want both dressers.
I want a bigger house.
I want to trade my '84 Ford
straight across for Bob Etta's '91 Prelude.
My husband wants some other family to own
    a pickup truck.

PART THREE

WHAT THE CLEANING LADY KNOWS

What The Cleaning Lady Knows

Cleanliness is not and never has been next to godliness.

White carpets are hell.

You can get by without Comet, Spic and Span or lemon oik,
but Windex is mandatory.

Ammonia can cause pneumonia.

People who pay to have houses cleaned are lonely.

Children whose parents work full-time will fall in love with you.

Rich people splatter diarrhea
on the inside rim of their toilet seats, just like the rest of us.

Cleaning rags should always be washed separately with
    bleach.

Cash is better than checks.

Down On My Knees

cleaning out my refrigerator
and thinking about writing a religious poem
that somehow combines feeling sorry for myself
with ordinary praise, when my nephew stumbles in for coffee
to wash down what looks like a hangover
and get rid of what he calls hot dog water breath.
I wasn't going to bake the cake

now cooling on the counter, but I found a dozen eggs tipped
sideways in their carton behind a leftover Thanksgiving
    Jell-O dish.
There's something therapeutic about baking a devil's
    food cake,
whipping up that buttercream frosting,
knowing your sisters will drip by and say Lord yes
they'd love just a little piece.

Everybody suffers, wants to run away,
is broke after Christmas, stayed up too late
to make it to church Sunday morning. Everybody should

drink coffee with their nephews,
eat chocolate cake with their sisters, be thankful
and happy enough under a warm and unexpected January sun.

Dear Dad

I wish I was there with you
drinking weak coffee, eating cheese,
crackers, canned tuna, pork rinds
and pickled pig's feet.

I want to sit with you
on the old back porch, chain-smoke
generic cigarettes till we find
every tuna fish can ashtray you own.

We could talk about Momma,
all the women you've known since
she's been gone, argue a bit
about religion, sex, drugs, and diabetes.

I wouldn't mention your desperate need
to see a doctor, because I know
how much you hate the sonofabitches.

Instead I'd say you look good
for a lonely, dried-up, 73-year-old man
who admits he would have takne
far better care of himself if he'd known
he was gonna live this long.

I miss Dillard, Dad. I miss Roseburg, Winston,
the swimmin' hole at Coon Hollow,

the South Umpqua River, stealing watermelons
from Burk's Blue Fruit Stand on hot summer nights,
and picking beans to help pay for school clothes.

All your North Bend/Coos Bay kids
are fine, and keeping plenty busy.
Monday I cleaned the church building,
Tuesday I cleaned at home. Wednesday
I taught a children's Bible class,
Tonight I have a class. But come Friday

I'll be happy on Highway 42,
Passing chip trucks in the rain, swerving
To miss mud slides, stopping in Remote
To get rid of coffee so I can buy more, and singing
with the radio, cruising through Camas Valley
hanging a right at Brockway Store . . .

Home Alone

Cigarette smokers,
sweet tooths,
alcoholics, teetotalers,
bad cooks, good cooks,
food stamp recipients,
low blood sugar and type 2 diabetes,
depression, codependency, cancer,
high energy, low self-esteem,
nap takers, neat freaks, control freaks,
carpal tunnel syndrome,
strong arms, skinny ankles, pot bellies,
public speakers, introverts, braggers,
blue eyes, long lets, red necks,
enablers, naggers, whiners,
pride, guilt and honesty all run in my family.
We have an out of work long haul truck driver,
a race car driver, a certified pesticide applicator,
an Olympic decathlon pole vault record breaker,
Sunday School teachers, a politician, a poet,
professional house cleaners, a dishwasher who
works in a dive for dimes, and an Environmental
Services worker who mops floors at the local hospital
and recently moved in with me because
paying off her ex's bills put her in a real bind and
even though she comes in from work exhausted
she manages to vacuum my carpets and Comet my toilets.
There's never a dull moment, though I'm praying for one,
that my sister will get her own place soon,

that my billiant, eighteen-year-old needs-to-get-a-job son
will snap out of it, that my in-laws place will hurry up
    and sell,
that they'll pack up and move to Arkansas already. . . .
    I see myself
Home alone writing a poem in a quiet house, smoking one
    cigarette
after another, eating candy, flicking
my ashes on the floor.

Mikey Likes It

the way I wait on him
hand and food, wash his hair
most morning, fry up hashbrowns,
mend his work jeans and in general
act interested even when I'm not.
Mikey likes back rubs, "Renegade" reruns,
Race cars, fishing poles, guns,
Beef jerky and a beefed-up truck.
He doesn't do dishes or yard work. He forgets
my birthdayand doesn't bring me flowers.
No candy. No sweet talk. But I know
he loves me. He pays the bills,
gives my grown boys bear hugs
and money when he sees a need.
Once he charged a new set of tires
for my sister's old car
because she's alone and poor.
If you need a place to stay,
Mikey will give you our key.

If He's Lucky

When his lower back goes out
Dad will lie down flat
on his living room floor,
raise his legs up
as high as he can
    (his hernia tucks back
into his groin),
and kind of swivel his feet
first one way, then the other, slowly.
If he's lucky
his pain goes away.

Frail, beanpole thin,
Dad thinks about dying.
He calls up the mental list of his life,
good things to one side,
bad things to the other, believing
the good outweighs the bad.
For just a moment
he thinks he'll make it
into heaven
as he lies there
feeling no pain
his cold hands folded
across his heart,
his feet up,
his eyes closed.

Old Bawling Hags

Lonely, horny, divorced,
a struggling, gross Christian
recently prescribed antibiotics
and nerve pills, hooked on nicotine,
caffeine and non-dairy creamer,
my sister says she's willing
to lower her standards, date a man
ugly as a mud fence
or stupid as a box of rocks,
so long as he has a kind heart.

Parked at a downtown 7-Eleven,
we share chili-cheese nachos,
a Big Gulp, and buy-two-
get-one-free pack of Sno balls.
Counting each other's gray hair and wrinkles,
We split a Moon Pie and cry.

Pre-Holiday PMS

I don't want to be thankful this year.
I don't want to eat turkey and I could care
if I never again tasted
your mother's cornbread stuffing.
I hate sweet potato pie. I hate mini marshmallows.
I hate doing dishes whil you watch football.

I hate Christmas. I hate name-drawing.
I hate tree-trimming, gift-wrapping,
and Rudolph the zipper-necked red-nosed reindeer.
I just want to skip the whole merry mess—
unless, of course, you'd like to try
to change my mind. You could start
by telling me I'm pretty and leaving me
your charge cards
and all your cash.

Sleeping with Dad

I was in the seventh grade.
That dark-haired woman from Coos Bay
And her two pretty but wicket teenage daughters
had finally moved out. I have no idea
where my sister Mary Beth had gone off to.
This was the year she started drinking.
I hated our tiny dark back bedroom, was afraid
to sleep alone in it.
Early evening, Dad slid the couch
out from the wall, let the back down, click.
The nerve
In Dad's lower back was pinched, and he said
he'd have to sleep non the couch for a few nights
because his bed springs where shot.
If you want, he said, unfolding the brown wool blanket,
you can sleep with me.

In the cold dark,
with all my clothes on, I slipped under
the scratchy wool, slowly inched toward him until
my toes were against the backs of his calves, my nose,
somewhere between his shoulder blades
smelling his musty stinky T-shirt smell.
For one long, wonderful week—
That smell I'd never before liked, that touch
I'd always wanted.

Menopause

I dreamed I had an alligator belly,
washboard hard. We're talking Schwarzenegger.
Now I've had my share of odd dreams,
gross dreams I've never told anyone about.
I've had nightmares that sat me straight up
and left every light in the house on.
I've had trapped in hell dreams,
a shopping downtown naked dream.
Never had a flying dream though,
and I think I'd like that.
Anyhow, I called my sister
and told her about my buffed belly dream,
how my fingers still felt numb from rubbing it over and
        over again,
how I felt scared and wondered what my friends would think.
My sister, who's in her second year of major menopause, said,
Oh Ginger Gay, that's nothing! I could fill buckets
With the sweat from all my horror dreams—
And you're calling me with a silly little hard belly dream?
It's nothing, trust me! Just put a shirt over it and get here
        quick
to help me cut off this huge, bloody growth
hanging out of my crotch.

Sadder Than a Beautiful Young Woman

with money,
a good man,
and cancer,
is my not so young,
not so beautiful sister
who's flat broke,
divorced
and has cancer.

Saddest of all is the fact
that I pussyfoot around
telling her that it's never too late
to let go and let God.
Wouldn't want to preach
her a sermon or anything.

I Punch Out Jesus,

Peter, Andrew, James, John
the empty net, and the net full of fish
from the visual aids packet
for my pre-schoolers' next Sunday School Lesson.

> *Questions:*
> *What were the fishermen doing when Jesus first*
>   *saw them?*
> *How many fish had they caught?*
> *What happened when Jesus told Peter to throw his*
>   *net into the water?*
> The kids will know the answers.

Tell me again about forever,
about that land of endless day,
that part about no pain,
no tears.

My Sister Believes in Miracles

The latest of which
is a short, bald, fifty-year-old Italian
with sciatic nerve damage in his left leg
resulting from his second or is it his third back surgery.
He's wonderful. They're a perfect match she tells me,
what with both of them being recovered
alcoholic / drug addicts, both
on the wagon for years now, both
having named their Higher Power. God, of course,
who first had to teach her once and for all
the heartbreak of lust combined with low self-esteem,
followed by the proverbial codependent marriage
and the subsequent births of children
she has no control over, whose fathers
are worthless, nowhere to be found
when their little girls cry in the middle of the night.
She's met his family, all responsible
come-from-old-money Italians.
One younger brother she says is drop-dead gorgeous.
It's crazy. It's amazing, she says,
A German marrying an Italian.
A neat freak versus a slob.
He makes his children mind.
He owns three cars, she says, Three!
He wants to pay my phone bill for God's sake.
Neither of us can cook.
He doesn't drink any more.
He believes in Jesus.

Backflip

There are beautiuflly wind-deformed pine trees
just at the edge of the cliffs here. And, the ocean—
its secret beaches I've been going to tell about
for the longest time now. Sand dollars, fat jellyfish,
anemone, yellow scotch broom in bloom, beach grass, stinky
seaweed, snails on salal leaves, hundreds of tiny sand fleas
    doing backflips.
There are so many wind, sand, and ocean-swept clean
    things. There is

my ex brother-in-law sitting cross-legged on my living
room floor
watching the local morning news, killing time before walking
in the rain to my oldest sister's house. He's going to build a
deck for her.
We all still love him, find odd jobs for him when he's in town.
He's still almost good-looking, but way too thin. He's lost
all his front teeth. He's finally off drugs, a beer drinker now.
Some days, he says, he'll go through half a case by noon.

Going Down

I'm scrubbing my back bathroom toilet
Because you never know when
Someone might stop by
And need to use it just when
Someone else has the main bath occupied.
It could happen.
I can't believe that my sister,
My best friend,
Married that old tightwad Italian
And moved away. I might as well
Scrub the tub while I'm on my knees.
My sister did call last week. She'd
Just come from visiting our dad
Who's still refusing medication
But wishes he had some more of those percodans
Like they gave him before
They amputated his leg. She said
Dad checked his blood sugar level
And it was up again, sky high.
He just wants to be left alone.
I can't believe the mold
That's grown on the title grout back here.
God. What a mess. That's me,
Straightening deck chairs on the Titanic,
Lining those loungers up perfect,
When there's souls to be saved,
And the ship is going down.

With a Wicked Little Jab

I stop / eject the Golden Oldies cassette
Of Jerry Lee Lewis singing *"goodness gracious,*
great balls of fire." I'm not in the mood
for a plast from the past or even the two bites of
   old-fashioned
microwaved oatmeal that I knew I couldn't eat
before I cooked it. I just wanted to act routine,
take a shower, get dressed, eat something, dust a
bookcase, burn
some paper trash, thank God for my day off.
Thought I'd clean out a closet, or maybe bake cookies.
But I can still feel yesterday's sun, yesterday's headache
the way I had nerve to whine about it
to whatever sister stood by me in our dad's yard as well
   watched
our brother mow the wet grass,
a cigarette hanging out of the corner of his mouth,
the way the mower kept dying, the way he patiently
bent down with a stick, tipped the mower
to knock clumped grass off the dull blades,
while, white-faced, our dad was throwing up
off the corner of the front porch, sitting bent over
in his wheel chair, trying not to get any on his one foot.
He wants us to believe that his surgeon saws off legs for
   money.
He's fired his diabertees doctor, hasn't had insulin for days,
Thinks Home Health care is a joke,

and told the Meals on Wheels folks to hit the road.
He says he wants to be alone. But
he gets scared, calls us up. So we come to mow his yard
and cook him meals that he can't keep down.
He wants to die at home.
And he wants us to be there when it happens.

Habitual Offender

My oldest sister sits
Eating a cracker at our dad's kitchen table.
Dad's false leg with its worn, black shoe,
lace undone, stands beside her next to the wall
by the window where gray light manages
to filter through the three-quarters shut miniblinds
stained yellow with cigarette smoke and gas fumes
from his stove's burners
which keep his little shack house way too hot. But Dad
says he'll never be warm again.
Our eyes burn and water every time we visit. Every weekend.
But, after twenty minutes or so, our eyes adjust,
And it's not so bad.
His drinking water smells.
We bring in bottled water for coffee, hide it under his sink
So we won't have to listen to him gripe
about how he's been drinking his water for going on
        twenty-six years now.
Diabetic ulcers have formed on the bottom and side
of his one foot. His toes are purple.
He suffered too much with his first amputation, he says,
To live through another one.
He's sleeping now. So we sit. My sister hands out
crackers, puts on some coffee. I'm wondering
if our brother will show up, but I'm thinking
he's holed up somewhere half-drunk, crying
in his beer, forty-five years old, waiting
for his old man to just once tell him that he loves him.

PART FOUR

NOT SLEEPING TOO GOOD MYSELF

Thanksgiving

Do not forget to entertain strangers, for by doing some
people have entertained angels without knowing it.
—Hebrews 13:2

If the almost perfectly fluted edge
of your homemade pumpkin pie's crust burns
even though you carefully crinkled aluminum foil
    around it
as soon as you noticed it was browning way too fast,
for goodness sake don't cry. Just cut it off.
Swirl Cool Whip around where the crust was.
Nobody really cares. They will eat it.
Life will go on, trust me. The truth is
There's always someone with a sadder story.

If your father hasn't had both his legs amputated,
if he isn't lying on a pee-stained mattress;
doesn't have bed sores, a diaper rash, a shriveling liver,
a bad heart and cataracts; if your sister
isn't burnt black from neck to groin
from radiation, if chemo
doesn't have her full phlegm and bile, trust me,
these are your good times.

The trick is keeping busy, cleaning house, cooking, opening
your door to strangers, entertaining all possible angels.

No Code*

I'm thankful that my brother wasn't drunk
When he found our dad dead in his own smelly bed.
My sister, coming in through the back door,
saw Dad dead first, but just kept walking
straight through to the kitchen to put on coffee, open
     curtains.
I'm thankful that my sister wasn't drunk,
That she's been sober for ten years now. Thank God.
Thank God it was my brother who closed Dad's eyes,
who called the appropriate authorities, chatting calmly
with my sister over coffee while they waited.

*a prearranged agreement for no life support

Not Sleeping Too Good Myself

My sister slips up and lets out
That's she's on sleeping pills.
Her welfare caseworker referred her to Mental Health.
They set her up with this counselor who
Prescribed 15mg. of flurazepam. Not sleeping
Too good myself, I'm thrilled for her.
The State seems plenty worried
About her getting a job—she looks like death,
Both her father and a sister have recently died,
She's married to, but not living with,
Some Catholic-Italian-Mafia-type.
They've convinced her that she's abusing her body,
Told her to try cutting down on caffeine,
And to eat a regular meal at least once a day.

She tells me that she's told them about God.
I'm not surprised. My sister, the caretaker:
Finally taking better care of herself, eating
Some hot meals, drinking way less coffee, sleeping
Half the night, putting in job applications, inviting
Her caseworker to come to church some Sunday.

I Try Not to Write Poems

about my dead sister's daughter's blocked fallopian tubes,
About how badly she wants to have a baby
But can't afford the corrective surgery right now.
Funerals are expensive.

I try not to write
About family, death,
Cancer, divorce, my nephew's autistic son, alcoholism,
Hepatitis C, insomnia, root canals—my dentist says I
    need two, or
I could have both teeth pulled and see an orthodontist, maybe
Get a partial.

I try not to think
About money, how I don't have enough
To pay for my son's careless driving ticket.
From a thousand miles away he tells me not to worry,
That he's too busy with Technical Writing to be driving
    anyway.
He's going to a Christian college to become an engineer
So that he can make lots of money and some day
Buy his momma a summer home by a lake somewhere
    Beautiful and peaceful

Where I could write poetry all day long.

About My Tenth Death Poem In a Row

I tell myself that I've got to stop this, get out
In a green meadow somewhere and talk to some dandelions,
Roll around in the grass, careful
Not to squish any little living thing.
Here's a long title for poem number eleven:
> *"Accidedntally killing Some Little Bugs*
> *When I Was Just Trying To Get Away*
> *From It All and Lie Down In A Quiet Meadow . . ."*
Well, it isn't going to happen. I don't have time to get away
Because I've taken on extra work so I won't have time
    to think
About my dead sister and father and everybody
Knows there is no clear escape from death—unless
God's got your name in the Book of Life. But I am not dead,
And after so many days I am no longer bawling
In grocery store aisles, and have actually begun to laugh
At stupid jokes on TV sitcoms.
Oh, I can keep writing death if I want to. I can feel sorry
For the little bugs, the ten or twelve out of however many
    zillions
That I might kill in some green place sometime if I want to.

Smoking and Drinking

Dad warns me
That there are approximately fourteen farts per cup of coffee.
But it's very important, he says, to get any and all poison
Build up out of a body. It's nothing to be ashamed of.
Your straight shot of whikey'll kill germs. Cigarette smoke
Is good too. It keeps bugs and general impurities out of
     the air.
And if it weren't for his baseball-sized hernia popping out
Everytime he lights up, he'd still be rolling his own.

Dad says he doesn't worry about anything.
When he goes to bed at night, he sleeps.
He tells me to get a second opinion
Before I go getting cut on for any female problems.
All doctors are quakcs, he says. Look at how many times
They've tried to kill me. Look how they killed your mother.

Time and Money

Monday. March 10th. Exactly
Two months since my sister died
And I'm depressed over how depressed I still am.
My husband asks what's the matter and I tell him
For God's sake it's only been two months.
He doesn't know what he can do for me,
So he chops kindling.
He's chopped enough to last well into winter.

I tell him it's not just death, it's everything—
My crappy cleaning jobs, my arthritis, my fuzzy perm.
Don't you ever feel old, I ask, don't you ever feel
Bad about your thinning hair? Nope, he says.
Doesn't bother me at all.
The sooner it all falls out the better.
Same with my teeth.

Corns and Bunions

Certainly, bunions are painful, hard
To live with, the reality of never again
Wearing your favorite high heels
Or any pretty shoes for that matter.
Oh my beautiful dresses,
My silky, slinky things that
Will now look as stupid as good manure,
Worn with ugly, flat, wide shoes.
There is a surgical procedure for bunions, but I'm chicken.
I'll just go orthopedic. Well, I shouldn't say just—
For Pete's sake, I'm only 40. Well, maybe I shouldn't say
Only. My mother died at 42. She didn't have bunions,
but she did have corns.

O Momma

I come from a real life
soap opera family
complete with death,
replacements, affairs, adoptions, abortions,
addicts, prison terms, love, etcetera.

They say we're a kind bunch
helping each other, and anyone hurting.
I think it's death
that's brought us so close.
Especially Momma's.

I remember Dad raising
the bushy eyebrow over his one good eye,
and telling us to be careful
of seeing only the good side of people.

But we're perceptive that way.
We know hurt.

Stuff

I was thinking it was just me with my
little ongoing sadnesses, regrets and poor life choices
combined with a sinus infection and PMS,
but it's looking like everybody is on the verge
of tears. Here I am, bloated, just waiting to start
bleeding like a stuck pig, with swollen eyelids
and nasal passages, praying for a post nasal drip,
with a huge pimple right in the middle of my forehead—
the kind you know better than to squeeze, smiling
anyway, when people around me are crying.
Well, some with just their eyes full, blinking rapidly.
Men, women, children, family, friends, and fellow Christians—
the normally on-top-of-things people are falling apart,
     breaking
down in front of me. Folks who've made good choices,
have good jobs, money to send their kids to private schools,
the best colleges. Women I know who are as pretty
on the inside as the outside, are crying to me for God's sake.
Do they think I have it together or something?
Is it my kind heart? Is that my problem? Don't they know
I'm a poet, that I'll write this stuff down?

The Gift

The preacher's sermon is on the parable of the talents.
His point is that God has given each of us at least one gift.
The challenge is to know what our gifts are.

Recovering from her third divorce,
A former bartender, a heavy smoker,
eater of half a dozen donuts at a time,
loudmouthed, interrupted,
big-hearted and God-fearing,
my sister says she knows what her one talent is:
Encouraging others.

God Comes In Handy

when you're recently divorced,
Oh so vulnerable, yet thankful
That you're nowhere near as lost as you once were,
Licking the couple of dandruff-like flakes of crank
Off your tongue-dampened finger
Because your nose is too raw to snort up
That last little bit.
When you're walking with your head down
Years later, clean and brutally sober,
When out of the clear blue
You practically step on this little square
Half gram of the stuff, chopped and ready,
Right there in your own front yard,
At the tip of your worn-out Reebok,
Glowing up out of the green grass.
Of course nobody is around,
So you pocket it. Stunned.
Down on your luck and money,
You know you could sell it,
Buy your mixed-up child new school clothes,
Pay your phone bill, or just portion it out
And mix it with your coffee
For who knows how many mornings.
Energy. Power! Yeah, right.
                              Shaky.
Your face pale in the mirror about the toilet,
You drop the shit and flush.

Crazy 'Bout a Mercury

As you know, my sister says, I talk to God
about everything. Lately I've talked a lot
about being poor, how I don't like it. Sure,
I know I'm not really poor, but, the thing is—
I know you already know this—
if you're with Him, He overlooks
your weaknesses whatever they may be
mine being greed and sex, as in, I want some
but can't have it right now. Sure, it's my own fault
for picking drunks and druggies for husbands, anyway
I got to thinkinbg about that Mustard Seed Faith,
how Jesus says, I tell you the truth,
if you have faith the size of a mustard seed
you can move mountains. Well,
you know how I've had nothing
but a string of junker cars that break down, blow up,
catch on fire,
and it struck me that all I gotta do is ask for a decent car.
If I asked for a brand spanking new Mercury,
I know God would give me one. Now
I'm not saying I'm gonna ask Him,
I figure I got a couple hundred miles left in my old
        Plymouth,
and, I'm learning to pray for what I really need,
not just for just for what I think I want, like sex.

A Man for Mary

One who wouldn't dream of insisting
that she pay her own car insurance,
buy her own food, and have sex every night
whether she's bathed or not.

A divorced man is OK—
she's divorced herslef, three times.
She used to drink, do drugs.
She was beaten once, locked up
for three nights.

Mary wants a Stable Sam kind of guy, a God-fearing
Responsible man who's got a house
She could help make a home. Maybe
one of those newer manufactured homes, but
she's had it with eighteen-foot tin cans that leak.

Mary loves house plants, lots of windows, lots of light.

December Sunday

Two of my sisters and I decide to skip Bible study
And drive to Roseburg in time to catch the worship
Services there, then go visit our unstable, still recovering
From Dad's death, still alcoholic brother, whom we love.
We stop for coffee, stop for gas, stop to use the sani-cans
At the covered bridge in Remote. We don't make it
In time for church. When we get to our brother's,
I fall asleep in his recliner.
He's hoping to come see us next weekend. He gives us
    the key
To our dad's place, a rundown shack we've put up for sale.
We go home along the way to tstop there
To get Dad's old orange hanging lamps for our niece.
She says they'll look perfect in her condominium.
We pick up cheeseburger baskets, decide to eat them at
    Dad's,
Like we used to, sitting around the dark brown Formica-
Chipped kitchen table with the green chairs.

The back door still sticks.
The kitchen faucet still drips.
We can still smell mold and urine.
It's so cold we see our breath.
Steam rises from our French-fries.
I mention that I'm just not feeling too well, probably
Getting that flu. My sisters can't get the hanging lamps
To come loose from the living room ceiling. It looks like

Dad screwed the stupid things up too tight. Maybe,
If the place doesn't sell, some spring
We'll come back and figure out how
To unscrew the ugly things, get them donw
Without tearing them up.

Sometimes A Cleaning Lady

gets to feeling sorry for herself, her reflection these days
in somebody else's floor-to-ceiling,
beveled, cherrywood framed to-die-for mirror,
her forty-something year-old not-so-blue anymore eyes,
that he pan stick makeup conceals only until
she begins perspiring in the indoor August heat;
her head in somebody else's oven, her toilet brush
scouring some rich retired doctor's mauve toilet
whose pale color exactly matches the tile
surrounding the large oval shaped Jacuzzi
with its gold faucets, spigot, and drain:
as she wipes the tiny blonde shaved hairs
stuck three quarters up the side of the tub, gently,
with Soft Scrub, so as not to scratch the surface.

She knows that she is trusted.
She knows that money and things
don't necessarily make you happier or prettier,
that she could turn
on the air conditioning, make herself
a sandwich if she wanted to. You wouldn't
believe what all she knows. Today she found a note
left on top of her check: Help yourself to a cold drink,
Sweetheart,
make yourself at home.

For everyone who exalts himself will be humbled, and he who humbles himself will be exalted.
—Luke 14:11

Biographical Note

Ginger Andrews was born and raised in North Bend, Oregon, and lives there still. She runs a small house cleaning business with her three sisters, who all live within walking distance. Her work has appeared in numerous anthologies, as well as in *Poetry, The American Voice, The Hudson Review, MARGIE, Ship of Fools, The Oregonian,* and *The Writer.* In 1997, she received the Mary Scheirman Poetry Award. She is a former secretary and janitor for the North Bend church of Christ, where she teaches Bible class to preschool children on Wednesday nights.